Reviews of Better Divorce Blueprint and Journal

Vicky Townsend:
Co-Founder and CEO The National Association of Divorce Professionals

"Wow! Do I wish I had this when I was going through my divorce! I never knew about divorce coaching when I was going through it, but boy would it have made a difference in the outcome of my divorce and my life. Her advice and experience will guide you through a complicated process and will save you heartache and money and will set you up for a better future. Do yourself and your family, especially your children, a big favor and take the time to do the work in this workbook. It will be the best investment you make as you embark on this journey."

Keli Hazel, CPA, Financial Planner and Author of *Suddenly Single*

"Man oh Man do I wish I had a Better Divorce Blueprint when I was going through my divorce. Methodical and a life saver come to mind. Will definitely recommend to my clients contemplating or in the throes of divorce. A necessity to get you started on the right track personally and financially."

Barbara Bell, Founder Bell Divorce Advisors, AIF, CDFA, CDS
Certified Divorce Financial Analyst

"Better Divorce Blueprint is a must read for anyone facing divorce, no matter which phase they're in. This easy read is an outline for protecting property, rights and your heart. The author looks at each phase of divorce from a place of love and patience, to help families move through the difficult process with ease and understanding."

Samantha Lennon, Partner Heredia & Lennon Family Law LLC, Family Law Attorney

"Paulette's comprehensive guide to divorce is a must-read for anyone who is contemplating or currently going through the divorce process. As a divorce attorney, I would recommend it to all of my clients without hesitation. Better Divorce Blueprint is a game changer."

Tierra Womack: MBA and Founder of The Brave Way
Confidence and Success Coach, Narcissist Abuse Expert

"This is a must read for anyone going through divorce as it blends real world advice, practical strategies and actionable exercises which leave the reader feeling empowered, believing that they too can come out better on the other side of divorce no matter what!"

Martin F Kane II : McGrath and Kane Inc., Esquire

"Anyone who is about to embark on a divorce needs to read this book prior to calling a divorce attorney! The insight that you will glean will save you thousands of dollars but as important, save you millions of emotional dollars. That the divorce attorney is not your therapist, is tremendous advice. Reading and understanding the contents of this book, will set you on the correct path.

It will allow you to avoid the inevitable pitfalls of divorce. It will give you the knowledge and power to press on through a very difficult and emotional period of your life. Things will get better. You need to take care of yourself mentally and physically during this process. Paulette gives you the path to get through what I refer to as the "emotional blender" of divorce. Following her keys to the mental, spiritual and physical betterment of yourself will allow you to wade through this process from a much healthier perspective."

Ilyssa Panitz: Editor: "5 Things You Need To Know To Survive And Thrive During and After a Divorce," Content Director for The National Association of Divorce Professionals, Divorce News Journalist

"'Better Divorce Blueprint' is not only invaluable for people going through a divorce but also for the professionals that serve them.

Anything and everything you can possibly think of and encounter during a divorce is jam packed into this book. Custody, financial, co-parenting, moving – it is all in there and I am just naming a few.

Paulette carefully takes you through each phase of "divorce" and teaches you what you need to know so you can make clear and better decisions to get the best possible outcome."

Sonia Queralt: Family Law Attorney, Co-Founder of Divorceify

"As a divorce litigator and having been divorced myself, Paulette's book is exactly the type of resource that clients need when going through the divorce process. Paulette does a wonderful job of breaking down the divorce process and delivers insights into all of the different emotions and issues that can arise when someone is going through divorce. The advice and tips that Paulette offers clients are insightful because she is a divorce professional that has also been through the divorce process herself. I cannot recommend this book enough – if you are starting the divorce process or are in the middle of it, this book will help you every step of the way. If you are a professional that works with divorcing clients – tell them to RUN and get this book NOW."

Tracy Ann Moore-Grant, Family Law Attorney and Founder Amicable Divorce Network

"Paulette is a caring and passionate divorce coach and mediator who has developed an innovative concept for helping individuals divorce better. As an experienced divorce professional, it is refreshing to see Paulette's ideas for helping parties move through the process and onto the next chapter of their life with positivity. This book is a must read for anyone facing divorce."

Winter Wheeler, Winter Wheeler Mediation & Arbitration LLC

"In Better Divorce Blueprint, Paulette Rigo tackles every aspect of divorce and lays the good, bad, and ugly on the table. Paulette makes clear that divorce is a complicated endeavor, but does so in a relatable, compassionate, and easy to understand way. Her empathy, understanding, and genuine desire to empower the divorcing is palpable. She pursues a holistic approach to divorce and advocates for preparation of the mind and heart, not just the paperwork. Paulette sparks joy and hope in moving on, showing that there is light and passion in being whole with or without a partner. This is a must read for anyone contemplating divorce."

Rebecca White

The work I've done in Better Divorce Blueprint as well as the year that I've worked with Paulette has transformed my life. I was a recently divorced stay at home mom who hadn't worked in my tech security field for 8 years. I didn't know what the next stage of my journey could be. A mutual friend said I should talk to Paulette. She challenged me to find the answers inside me and pointed me in the right direction.

Over the course of a year, Paulette helped me take an idea and nurture it into a business. She empowers me and validates my efforts. I went from being confused and anxious to feeling completely in control of my destiny. I couldn't have done that without Paulette's special style of coaching. She takes the time to understand where her clients are and meets them there. It's been one of the best experiences of my life and, thanks to Paulette, I'm ready for the new adventure ahead!

BETTER DIVORCE
BLUEPRINT
JOURNAL

A PERSONAL LETTER FROM PAULETTE

Well hello gorgeous woman and welcome to the Better Divorce Blueprint Journal!

I'm so excited to have you as a part of my community of gorgeous, intelligent, brave women with a passion for creating a better divorce from start to finish (and Yes beyond!).

Let me tell you a little bit about me before we embark on this journey together because it's really important for your success in this program that you know me and you trust that I know what you are going through and how much I truly understand.

I am a survivor of an eight year fully litigated and appellate divorce process and since that time I have helped hundreds of women just like you to come out the other side whole and secure.

Better Divorce Academy was born out of my desire to change the landscape of the divorce process to uplevel the experience to result in a better process and outcome for all members of each family and my clients. It's my mission and my purpose to remove as much of the pain for you as you walk through each and every step of the divorce process, to help you avoid the same pitfalls and mistakes that I've made and to show you opportunities and shortcuts that took me years to learn.

But it's not going to be easy. No divorce journey is.

Take a slow deep breath, know that you will be supported and get ready for a very liberating and empowering experience.

This journal has been designed to be used in conjunction with the Better Divorce Blueprint course by Paulette Rigo. As such there will be references throughout to lesson numbers to help the course students.

However, you can use this without the course and still find it very useful.

If you would like to find out more about the course, please visit **BetterDivorceAcademy.com**

CHAPTER ONE
THERE IS A LOT TO TAKE INTO CONSIDERATION: GO SLOW

WHY ARE YOU CONTEMPLATING DIVORCE

1. Why is your marriage feeling like you are wearing shoes that don't fit?

_____

_____

_____

_____

_____

2. What makes your marriage uncomfortable?

_____

_____

_____

_____

_____

3. What makes it painful?

_____

_____

_____

_____

4. What makes it difficult?

_____

_____

_____

_____

_____

5. Are you arguing about petty things- like putting the toilet seat down?

_____

_____

_____

_____

6. Are you ignoring each other?

_____

_____

_____

7. Are you keeping secrets?

_____

_____

_____

8. Are you living parallel lives?

_____

_____

_____

9. Do you see 'eye to eye' on anything?

_____

_____

_____

10. Do you speak different love languages? (gifts, acts of service, words, quality time, touch)

_____

_____

_____

11. Or are you too similar and butt heads?

_____

_____

_____

12. It's important to have a private place you can keep your thoughts...do you have one?

_____

_____

_____

13. Have you shared your feelings with anyone?

_____

_____

_____

14. Do you trust anyone?

_____

_____

_____

15. You can trust yourself and you can trust me. This is why you are here. Do you agree?

_____

_____

_____

16. I ask that you begin to allow yourself the honor of FEELING your feelings. Make a list of your current feelings you are feeling right now.

_____

_____

_____

_____

_____

_____

17. Your gut is your second brain. It's much smarter than you give it credit for. How is your health, wellness, diet and sleep?

_____

_____

_____

_____

_____

_____

_____

18. What are the feelings in your gut telling you?

_____

_____

_____

_____

_____

_____

_____

19. What do you truly want? If you could wave a magic wand what would your future look like one year from now? Five years from now?

_____

_____

_____

_____

_____

_____

_____

20. Are you or your children in any danger?

_____

_____

_____

_____

_____

_____

_____

Your Thought Process

NEXT... CONSIDER A FEW QUESTIONS TO JOURNAL ABOUT YOUR THOUGHTS ON YOUR DISCONTENT.

1. What are the patterns that keep showing up?

_____

_____

_____

_____

2. What is your gut telling you?

_____

_____

_____

_____

3. Can you see how important this is now?

_____

_____

_____

_____

4. What feel familiar in your relationship?

_____

_____

_____

_____

5. Are you following someone else's ambiguous advice?

_____

_____

_____

_____

6. Is your gut information solid or in limbo?

_____

_____

_____

_____

_____

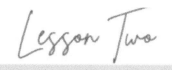

Lesson Two

Feel Your Feelings

LEARN HOW TO BREAK UP BETTER – TO LEAVE YOU AND THOSE YOU LOVE FREE TO MOVE FORWARD WITH OPEN AND FULLY HEALED HEARTS.

1. How do your feelings affect your life?

_____

_____

_____

_____

_____

_____

2. How do you deal with emotions?

•   anger?

_____

_____

_____

- betrayal?

- loss?

- shock?

- numbness?

- control?

- confusion?

_____

_____

_____

- panic?

_____

_____

_____

3. Are you ignoring your partner? Are they ignoring you?

_____

_____

_____

_____

4. Are you living parallel lives… If so for how long?

_____

_____

_____

WHAT EMOTIONS ARE YOU FEELING? HOW ARE THESE EXPERIENCES MAKING YOU FEEL? HOW ARE YOU COPING WITH THEM?

Emotion:

_____

_____

_____

_____

_____

Emotion:

_____

_____

_____

_____

_____

Emotion:

_____

_____

_____

_____

Emotion:

_____

_____

_____

_____

Deciding What You Want

WHAT CAN YOU LIVE WITH AND WHAT DO YOU NEED TO PROTECT AND SECURE YOUR FUTURE?

What would an ideal setting be for you and your spouse and if you have **children ...what is in their best interest**? Describe the ideal thinking about the following:

- Continuity?

- Bedrooms?

- Space?

- Commute from one parent to the other?

- Schools?

- Friends?

The financial and residential logistics can take some time to work out an ideal and affordable plan...**so it's time to think about what you want.**

1. Do you want to stay in the marital home or does your spouse want to stay in the marital home?

_____

_____

_____

2. How is equity divided?

_____

_____

_____

3. Have you tried to FIX communication conflicts?

_____

_____

_____

4. Are you both on board and totally transparent?

_____

_____

_____

5. Are you both financially aware of all your assets and liabilities?

_____

_____

_____

_____

_____

6. Are you with the same page on co-parenting schedules?

_____

_____

_____

_____

_____

CHECKLIST

CHECK THE ITEMS IN THIS LIST OF SIGNS THERE IS CONFLICT IN YOUR MARRIAGE

- ☐ You aren't having sex anymore

- ☐ You have little to say to each other

- ☐ You are with each other…but not really with each other

- ☐ You are actively ignoring your gut intuition telling you something is dreadfully wrong

- ☐ You are preoccupied with other peoples' needs and problems

- ☐ The distance between you keeps growing - and you are waiting to get help

- ☐ You fantasize about life without your spouse

- ☐ You've stopped fighting

- ☐ You have one or more relationship destroyers (criticism, defensiveness, contempt, stonewalling)

- ☐ You don't feel heard (and you might not be listening)

- ☐ You are on the verge of having an emotional affair

- ☐ You're going to your friends instead of your partner

- ☐ You don't like spending quality time together…drift away at parties, get home and go to your own corners, rather be apart

- ☐ Date nights are a thing of the past

- ☐ You are not each other's priority anymore

- ☐ You're feeling controlled

- ☐ Your partner is unwilling to get help or work on your relationship

Are any of these behaviors familiar?

_____

_____

_____

_____

_____

_____

What is your price of exit? What are you willing to let go of?

_____

_____

_____

_____

_____

_____

_____

What is non-negotiable for you?

_____

_____

_____

_____

_____

_____

_____

Being Responsible For Yourself

THESE STRATEGIES CAN HELP YOU MANAGE YOUR EMOTIONS EFFECTIVELY:

- ☐ Find your support system

- ☐ Identify friends or family members who can offer objective

- ☐ Helps to have a wise, non-attached external voice

- ☐ Give your support people the freedom to speak honestly

- ☐ Face your emotions

- ☐ Allow the emotional responses to come

- ☐ Every challenge is there for your increased wisdom

- ☐ It isn't necessary to over-analyze why you're feeling a certain way

- ☐ Celebrate your strengths

- ☐ Your strengths aren't to be brushed aside

- ☐ Openly acknowledging your strengths helps you subconsciously believe in yourself

- ☐ Offer emotional support to others

- ☐ When you support others, you're required to be straightforward and honest

- ☐ Helping others work through challenges

- ☐ Surround yourself with positivity

- ☐ Catch yourself in negative self-talk

- ☐ Engage in activities you enjoy

- ☐ Your commitment to a positive mindset reinforces your ability to be impartial and fair

Lesson Five

Dealbreakers

CHECKLIST OF BEHAVIORAL PATTERNS TO NOTICE:

☐ Conditional Love: behavior determines love received?

☐ Silent Treatment: time periods of silence, disregard

☐ Toxic Shame: feelings of guilt, duty or shame

☐ Crazy Making: provoking bad feelings through words or actions

☐ Manipulation: talking others into submission or twisting facts and situations

☐ Triangulation: using others to communicate through (flying monkeys)

☐ Minimizing/Demeaning: use of mockery and humiliation

☐ Gaslighting: Your reality is consistently denied or minimized (what are you talking about?)

☐ Future Faking: Everything will get better but never does

☐ Invalidation and criticism: You are not good enough

☐ Smear campaign: Demean and ruin your reputation

☐ Play victim: Want others to feel bad for them

☐ Refusing to take no for an answer

☐ Ghost you: Disappear for periods of time

How to Prepare and Protect Yourself

THIS CHECKLIST WILL BE A REFERENCE FOR YOU THAT YOU CAN CHECK OFF AS YOU COMPLETE EACH ITEM:

- ☐ It's very important that you secure your residential property; that includes your computer.

- ☐ Security system: "Nest" type system. Perhaps you have seen a few brands of very affordable cameras online or in Staples, Office Max type stores? It's not unusual to have mail stolen before, during or even after divorce.

- ☐ Place a camera where your mail is delivered. Consider a PO Box for Legal Documents.

- ☐ Shore up your financial position so you enter the divorce process prepared and on level ground.

- ☐ Change ALL login and passwords: email, cell phone, credit cards, bank accounts etc.

- ☐ Open new accounts in your own name.

- ☐ Establish private communication: NEW email.

- ☐ Remain vigilant and aware of subtle nuances.

- ☐ Delete social media (80% of evidence in divorce comes from social media).

- ☐ Stay OFF social media.

- ☐ Secure all accounts as single/solo account holders.

- ☐ Know exactly where all your valuables are and secure them.

- ☐ Make a list of your valuables.

- ☐ Change locks on doors.

- ☐ Do not share keys or codes.

- ☐ Stay calm and quiet, avoid gossip.

- ☐ Do not change your habits, friends or demeanor

CHAPTER TWO

Lesson One

How to Honor Your Values

Take the whole list of "values" and circle the most important 25 to you. What do you value most?

And then once you have them narrowed down…highlight your top 6.

LIST OF VALUES

Acceptance	Connection	Exploration
Accomplishment	Consciousness	Expressive
Accountability	Consistency	Fairness
Accuracy	Contentment	Family
Achievement	Contribution	Famous
Adaptability	Control	Fearless
Alertness	Conviction	Feelings
Altruism	Cooperation	Ferocious
Ambition	Courage	Fidelity
Amusement	Courtesy	Focus
Assertiveness	Creation	Foresight
Attentive	Creativity	Fortitude
Awareness	Credibility	Freedom
Balance	Curiosity	Friendship
Beauty	Decisive	Fun
Boldness	Decisiveness	Generosity
Bravery	Dedication	Genius
Brilliance	Dependability	Giving
Calm	Determination	Goodness
Candor	Development	Grace
Capable	Devotion	Gratitude
Careful	Dignity	Greatness
Certainty	Discipline	Growth
Challenge	Discovery	Happiness
Charity	Drive	Hard work
Cleanliness	Effectiveness	Harmony
Clear	Efficiency	Health
Clever	Empathy	Honesty
Comfort	Empower	Honor
Commitment	Endurance	Hope
Common sense	Energy	Humility
Communication	Enjoyment	Imagination
Community	Enthusiasm	Improvement
Compassion	Equality	Independence
Competence	Ethical	Individuality
Concentration	Excellence	Innovation
Confidence	Experience	Inquisitive

Insightful	Present	Stability
Inspiring	Productivity	Status
Integrity	Professionalism	Stewardship
Intelligence	Prosperity	Strength
Intensity	Purpose	Structure
Intuitive	Quality	Success
Irreverent	Realistic	Support
Joy	Reason	Surprise
Justice	Recognition	Sustainability
Kindness	Recreation	Talent
Knowledge	Reflective	Teamwork
Lawful	Respect	Temperance
Leadership	Responsibility	Thankful
Learning	Restraint	Thorough
Liberty	Results-oriented	Thoughtful
Logic	Reverence	Timeliness
Love	Rigor	Tolerance
Loyalty	Risk	Toughness
Mastery	Satisfaction	Traditional
Maturity	Security	Tranquility
Meaning	Self-reliance	Transparency
Moderation	Selfless	Trust
Motivation	Sensitivity	Trustworthy
Openness	Serenity	Truth
Optimism	Service	Understanding
Order	Sharing	Uniqueness
Organization	Significance	Unity
Originality	Silence	Valor
Passion	Simplicity	Victory
Patience	Sincerity	Vigor
Peace	Skill	Vision
Performance	Skillfulness	Vitality
Persistence	Smart	Wealth
Playfulness	Solitude	Welcoming
Poise	Spirit	Winning
Potential	Spirituality	Wisdom
Power	Spontaneous	Wonder

MY TOP SIX VALUES

_____

_____

_____

How does it feel to clearly know your top values?

_____

_____

_____

_____

_____

Can you see how knowing these and having them clearly in your sight will assist you along the way in making better decisions?
And getting through times of turmoil and confusion?

_____

_____

_____

_____

_____

REALITY TEST QUESTIONS:

- What is happening now that tells you this is important to you?

_____

_____

_____

_____

_____

- What are you tolerating by not moving on this issue?

_____

_____

_____

_____

_____

_____

- What have you attempted in order to resolve this?

- What feedback are you getting from your environment, health, friends, family, etc.?

- Who on your team can help?

_____

_____

_____

_____

_____

_____

- What obstacles are in your way?

_____

_____

_____

_____

_____

- What are your beliefs about achieving this outcome?

_____

_____

_____

_____

_____

_____

- What can you learn from someone who has already achieved this?

_____

_____

_____

_____

_____

_____

_____

WHAT ARE YOUR OPTIONS?

- What options are available to you?

_____

_____

_____

_____

_____

_____

- What could you do if you were without fear?

_____

_____

_____

_____

_____

_____

- What could you do if you were not answerable to anyone?

_____

_____

_____

_____

_____

_____

_____

- What could you do if time or money was not a constraint?

_____

_____

_____

_____

_____

_____

_____

- What could you do if the most important outcome was to learn more about yourself?

_____

_____

_____

_____

_____

_____

- What do you need to believe to open your options even more?

_____

_____

_____

_____

_____

_____

- How are your values being expressed or not being expressed by your actions, thoughts and feelings?

_____

_____

_____

_____

_____

_____

_____

Lesson Two

How to Tell The Children

CONSIDERATIONS FOR PARENTING PLAN

Make some notes on these considerations and how they apply to you

1. Distance between homes

---

2. Nesting: kids stay in same house and parents shift

---

3. Ability of parents to be civil and respectful to each other

---

---

4. Ability of parents to communicate effectively

---

5. Support system in place of both parents

_____

_____

_____

_____

6. Financial means

_____

_____

_____

_____

7. Based on this evaluation, What realistic expectation can be created?

_____

_____

_____

_____

How To Decide What is Right For You

Let's now consider how your own personal story and experience can play a role in your own divorce. It's never easy to separate our own history from our marriage. Answer the questions honestly, you may be surprised at the emotional baggage you still carry.

1. Did you come from a divorced family? What was its impact on you?

_____

_____

_____

_____

2. Did you have friends who were from divorced families? How did that affect you?

_____

_____

_____

_____

3. Did you grow up with messages about what divorce meant? What were those messages?

_____

_____

_____

_____

4. Did you discuss divorce with your spouse when you were dating?

_____

_____

_____

_____

_____

5. Is your spouse from a divorced family?

_____

_____

_____

_____

_____

6. What messages did their experience bring into your marriage?

_____

_____

_____

_____

_____

7. What role if any did religion play?

_____

_____

_____

_____

8. What role did TV/Movies play in your ideals about divorce?

_____

_____

_____

_____

9. What emotions and fears do you have about what others will think about you and your children?

_____

_____

_____

_____

10. Are you afraid of "what the neighbors will think?"

_____

_____

_____

_____

_____

11. Are you afraid of "what your family will think?" Or your spouse's family?

_____

_____

_____

_____

_____

12. Are you able to let go of other's opinions and judgments?

_____

_____

_____

_____

_____

How To End a Marriage

VISUALIZE AND CONTEMPLATE ON AN ISSUE YOU'VE STRUGGLED WITH FOR A LONG TIME AND INCLUDE HOW LONG YOU HAVE BEEN STRUGGLING WITH IT.

ISSUE:

_____

_____

_____

1. What emotions are you experiencing and name them?

_____

_____

_____

2. What are some common thoughts that show up when you think about this situation?

_____

_____

_____

3.   What emotions do you experience when you think these thoughts?

_____

_____

_____

_____

It may be one thought or several thoughts (i.e. I can't handle/stand this. Why is this happening to me? I'm a failure. Nothing goes right for me. What if I don't get past this? What if I lose everything?)

What are Your Thoughts on the Mindfulness Exercise?

_____

_____

_____

_____

_____

_____

_____

_____

_____

LET'S REPEAT THE OPTIONS EXERCISE NOW WITH MORE CLARITY:

1. What options are available to you?

_____

_____

_____

_____

_____

_____

2. What you could do if you were without fear?

_____

_____

_____

_____

_____

_____

3. What could you do if you were not answerable to anyone?

4. What could you do if time or money was not a constraint?

5. What could you do if the most important outcome was to learn more about yourself?

_____

_____

_____

_____

_____

_____

6. What do you need to believe to open up your options even more?

_____

_____

_____

_____

_____

_____

NOW LET'S CONSIDER SOME FORWARD THINKING QUESTIONS

1. Which one of your options will bring you one step closer to your desired outcome?

2. What actions do you need to take?

3. Is there anything you need to do before taking these actions?

4. How do you know that you are committed?

_____

_____

_____

_____

_____

5. By what date will you have completed the action(s)?

_____

_____

_____

_____

_____

6. What resources will you need to do this?

_____

_____

_____

_____

7. Do you need to tell anyone about your commitment?

_____

_____

_____

_____

8. What are your obstacles? How will you address them and when is your deadline?

_____

_____

_____

_____

9. On a scale of 1-10 (1=poor, 10=excellent) How do you rate yourself on each of the following? Commitment to action, Enthusiasm, Excitement, Certainty

_____

_____

_____

_____

10. What do you need to change to answer all the above with a 10?

_____

_____

_____

_____

_____

Negative and Positive Labels:

It's time to think of the labels you often apply to yourself and write them down. Write down your top 8 for your best and worst.

At my worst I am....

_____

_____

_____

_____

_____

_____

At my best I am...

_____

_____

_____

_____

_____

_____

FIVE GROWTH QUESTIONS:

1. Describe the current situation.

_____

_____

_____

_____

_____

_____

_____

2. How is this challenging you now?

_____

_____

_____

_____

_____

_____

_____

3. How would you like the situation to be?

_____

_____

_____

_____

_____

_____

4. How is this important to you, your purpose and your values?

_____

_____

_____

_____

_____

_____

5. What is the specific outcome you are looking for once this is resolved?

_____

_____

_____

_____

_____

_____

_____

CHAPTER THREE
IT'S OK TO LET YOUR OCD KICK IN: YOU CAN NEVER BE TOO PREPARED

WHAT YOU **CAN** DO BEFORE FILING

- YOU can do your research.
- YOU can be prepared.
- YOU can be organized.
- YOU can gather your facts.
- YOU can have a copy of every document.

YOU CAN NEVER BE TOO PREPARED

Here are a few **categories to create in your planner** that you will want to make note of that are not direct communication with professionals but having them all in one spot will be very helpful.

1. Financial payments that are late IE child support of spousal support. Keep track of the date you were supposed to receive it, the date you actually received it and if you NEVER received it.

Payment Type	Date Due	Date Received

2. Expenses that your soon to be ex (STBX) is supposed to reimburse you for. (medical expenses, utilities, maintenance, real estate taxes…etc.)

Expense	Notes	Date

3. All spending you incur to prove your budget (along with bank statements and credit card statements

4. Unusual or concerning activity, behavior and communication. (where, who, when and if anyone else witnessed it too)

Behavior	Who was there	Date/Place

5. Parenting time changes or alterations. Keep note of all dates and deviations.

Change	Notes	Date

6. All verbal attacks, criticisms and passive aggressive communication. Make note if the children were present, within earshot, if others were present or if you were alone.

Behavior	Who was there	Date/Place

7. Any parenting irregularities and failures: IE late or early exchanges, no shows, interference, complaining. And if the other parent also participated in or attended school conferences, sporting events, plays, doctor appointments…etc.

Parenting failures	Where	Date/Time

8. What your children say repeating what the other parent said or told them.

Comment from child   Date

_____   _____

_____   _____

_____   _____

_____   _____

_____   _____

9. If you are still living together: it's helpful to LOG the details of parenting functions: bathing, hygiene, meal preparation, drove to school, help with homework, signed teacher and doctor notifications, filled out camp and medical records.

_____

_____

_____

_____

_____

_____

_____

_____

10. If one parent is often missing, late, not home...make note of what time they left and when they returned home.

11. **Make note of** ANYTHING else that feels noteworthy or important. Trust me…you will forget. You may never need it or look at it again…but it could be important and will save you so much stress trying to recall when your mind is overwhelmed and in a state of fight or flight.

Lesson One

Ignorance Is Not Bliss

CHECK LIST OF ESSENTIALS

- ☐ Will
- ☐ POA
- ☐ HCP
- ☐ Mortgage
- ☐ Title
- ☐ Deed
- ☐ Insurance: Home, Car, Health and Life
- ☐ Bank Accounts
- ☐ Investments
- ☐ Retirement Accounts
- ☐ Do you need a Safety Deposit Box? Do you know where the key is?
- ☐ Is there cash in the house?
- ☐ Do you know where your valuable art, jewelry, furnishings are?
- ☐ Do you have receipts and documentation (photographs) of everything?

OTHER IMPORTANT DOCUMENTS TO HAVE MADE A COPIES AND PICTURES OF:

- ☐ Birth Certificates
- ☐ Driver's license
- ☐ Passports (Children's too)
- ☐ Social security cards

Importance of a Budget

DO YOU HAVE A BUDGET? (YES/NO)

FINANCIAL STATEMENTS

- Do you know all your living expenses that you incurred during the marriage?

_____

_____

_____

- Do you know your spending habits?

_____

_____

_____

- Do you know your spouse's spending habits?

_____

_____

_____

- Where do you buy gas?

_____

_____

_____

- What do you purchase at coffee shops?

_____

_____

_____

- How much money does your spouse typically spend on gifts? On vacations?

_____

_____

_____

- How often do you eat out?

_____

_____

_____

_____

- Do you choose the least expensive item on the menu? The most?

_____

_____

_____

_____

How to Choose Advocates

Who will be my advocates and what will they offer?

Possible Advocates:

_____   _____
_____   _____
_____   _____
_____   _____
_____   _____
_____   _____
_____   _____
_____   _____
_____   _____
_____   _____
_____   _____
_____   _____
_____   _____
_____   _____

BEST ADVOCATES:

Name: _____

About our relationship: _____

_____

_____

Contact:

_____

Name: _____

About our relationship: _____

_____

_____

Contact: _____

_____

Name: _____

About our relationship: _____

_____

_____

Contact: _____

_____

Name: _____

About our relationship: _____

_____

_____

Contact: _____

_____

Name: _____

About our relationship: _____

_____

_____

Contact: _____

_____

Name: _____

About our relationship: _____

_____

_____

Contact: _____

_____

Who is my number one advocate?

_____

Why?

_____

_____

_____

_____

_____

CHAPTER FOUR
YOU ONLY HAVE YOU TO TAKE CARE OF YOU

Managing Stress

MAKE A LIST OF YOUR PHYSICAL SYMPTOMS AND HEALTH GOALS.

Physical Symptoms

_____

_____

_____

_____

Health Goals

_____

_____

_____

ASK YOURSELF WHAT YOUR TOUCHPOINTS ARE.

Notice your triggers. Just notice and don't judge. Tears and anger are okay, but don't be caught off guard if your spouse tries to present you in a negative light.

How are you going to react if this happens?

_____

_____

_____

_____

_____

Can you witness your emotions without overreacting and adding fuel to the fire?

_____

_____

_____

_____

_____

Write down a common situation that happens, how you may react and how you would prefer to react.
Situation

_____

_____

_____

76

Your expected reaction

How you would prefer to react

IT IS TIME TO CREATE A STRESS MANAGEMENT PLAN THAT IS IN YOUR BEST INTEREST.

1. How can you best do that?

2. What is it that allows you to deal with stress successfully in the past?

3. What tools do you have?

4. What examples do you have?

_____

_____

_____

_____

5. How have you best handled stress in the past?

_____

_____

_____

_____

What legacy of composure and grace do you want to leave behind?

_____

_____

_____

_____

Caring for Mind & Body

How do you step back and care for yourself when you are experiencing so much stress and overwhelm?

_____

_____

_____

_____

_____

_____

Can you think of a time when you were in a stressful situation and you managed to handle it well?

- What was the situation?

_____

_____

_____

_____

- How did you manage it?

- How did it make you feel?

- What was the outcome of your ability to handle it?

Lesson Six

Be Creative with Your Future

Let's walk through these questions that will help you consider your future together.

- What brought you joy in the past?

_____

_____

_____

_____

_____

- What do you want your life to look like in the future?

_____

_____

_____

_____

_____

- How do you view change?

_____

_____

_____

_____

_____

_____

_____

- How can you simplify your life to allow yourself to feel calm, centered and prepared for each day?

_____

_____

_____

_____

_____

_____

_____

- Who do you want to be in the future?

_____

_____

_____

_____

_____

_____

- How do you want to look back at this experience 10 years from now?

_____

_____

_____

_____

_____

_____

1. Can you see how you have more control over your future than you thought you did?

_____

_____

2. Can you see how having a clear sight and vision of your future is helpful?

_____

_____

3. How do you feel now that you can visualize, internalize and realize the future you desire is real?

_____

_____

_____

_____

_____

_____

_____

What changes can you make to manage your stress levels?

_____

_____

_____

_____

_____

Name and describe 3 changes you're ready to implement.

Change 1:

_____

_____

_____

_____

Change 2:

_____

_____

_____

_____

Change 3:

_____

_____

_____

_____

What do you desire for your future

_____

_____

_____

_____

_____

CHAPTER FIVE
GET FAMILIAR WITH
THE PROCESS

QUESTIONS TO ASK BEFORE DECIDING WHICH PROCESS IS BEST FOR YOU

- How will your spouse deal with the prospect of divorce after the initial emotional impact has diminished? Will they be a bully, a "my way or the highway" negotiator or will they try to be fair and listen to all sides before deciding?

_____

_____

_____

_____

- How do you want to look back and remember how you were during the divorce process? Do you want to be angry and emotional or as someone who is credible and a good communicator?

_____

_____

_____

_____

- Are there considerations that are important to you such as privacy from public disclosure, or involvement in the decision- making process, or focus on children, participation by both parties or length of the process or control of the pace of the process or emotional impact that would dictate a preference of process for you?

_____

_____

_____

_____

_____

_____

- Do you want to be a client who partners with your spouse through mediation or do you need a buffer, like an attorney between you and your spouse?

_____

_____

_____

_____

_____

_____

- Do you want to be actively involved in the decision-making or do you want to give the power of decision making over to your attorney and let him or her loose to get a "win" for your side?

_____

_____

_____

_____

_____

_____

- How do you want to model effective behavior to others, your children, your family, or your community?

_____

_____

_____

_____

_____

_____

- How do you envision redefining the relationship with your spouse after the divorce is over – will you be co-parents, former spouses now still loyal to both of your families or will you cut all ties with his family and the communities you shared together?

_____

_____

_____

_____

_____

_____

- What are you most afraid of during the divorce process? How would you expect the attorney to engage with you in this?

_____

_____

_____

_____

_____

_____

- What kind of relationship do you want to have with your attorney?

_____

_____

_____

_____

_____

_____

- What is important to you in any business relationship? Do you want top notch service or do you want options as to how you can use their services more cost effectively? Do you want to be a partner with that person or just have them lead the process?

_____

_____

_____

_____

_____

_____

_____

PEOPLE INVOLVED IN THE DIVORCE PROCESS

How does it feel to know more of the players in the process?

_____

_____

_____

Who do you believe you need to help you and your children?

_____

_____

_____

_____

_____

_____

_____

CHAPTER SIX
LASTING IMPRESSIONS LAST A LIFETIME

WHAT ARE YOUR IMPRESSIONS OF DIVORCE?

1. Did your parents stay together?

2. Are they still married?

3. Did they stay together for the children?

4. Did they divorce?

5. Did they involve you in their pains and decisions?

_____

_____

6. How did you and your siblings handle the changes?

_____

_____

7. Did you take sides?

_____

_____

8. Did they alienate you from the other parent?

_____

_____

9. Did you have friends whose parents divorced?

_____

_____

10. How did they cope?

_____

_____

_____

_____

_____

_____

11. How did that make you feel?

_____

_____

_____

_____

_____

_____

Custody and Parenting Plans

MAKE NOTES ON SOME GUIDELINES FOR THESE IMPORTANT TOPICS

1. Babysitters? Nannies?

_____

_____

_____

2. Bedtime: how late is too late? Co-sleeping?

_____

_____

_____

3. Breast feeding?

_____

_____

_____

4. Cell phones?

_____

_____

_____

5. Chores? Allowance?

_____

_____

_____

6. Circumcision?

_____

_____

_____

7. Diet/Meals: snacks? sugar/candy? rigid meal times? eat on the sofa watching TV? vegetarian, vegan?

_____

_____

_____

8. Education: preschool, public versus private? boarding school?

_____

_____

_____

9. Holidays: where to spend them? how to spend them? celebrate or not? how much to spend on gifts?

_____

_____

_____

10. Homework: Do they have to do their homework to go outside and play? Video games?

_____

_____

_____

11. How much to spend on children's clothes? Consignment? Donations?

_____

_____

_____

12. Playdates? How often? How long? How many?

_____

_____

_____

13. Religion: different religions, go to church, not go to church? religious education?

_____

_____

_____

14. Sleepovers? Birthdays?

_____

_____

_____

15. Sports and Activities: How many is too many? What sports are safe? How much is too much to spend?

_____

_____

_____

16. Vaccinations? Anti-vac? Flu-shots?

_____

_____

_____

17. What to name the children? Family names? Unusual names? Common names?

_____

_____

_____

18. Vacations? Where to go? When to go? How much to spend? Who comes with us?

_____

_____

_____

19. Pets? No pets? Cat? Dog? Both? Snake?

_____

_____

_____

20. Video games? Social media? Internet usage?

_____

_____

_____

Parenting Plan Options

You can see a range of templates at https://betterdivorceacademy.com/resources :

What type of plan will work best for our family?

☐ Alternating Weeks

_____

_____

_____

☐ Alternating Weeks and Midweek Visit

_____

_____

_____

☐ Alternating Weeks and Midweek Overnight

_____

_____

_____

☐ Alternating Every Two Days

_____

_____

_____

_____

☐ 2-2-3 Rotation

_____

_____

_____

_____

☐ 3-3-4-4 Rotation

_____

_____

_____

_____

☐ 5-2-2-5 Rotation

_____

_____

_____

_____

How To Support The Kids

CHILD SUPPORT

What are the rules in my state?

_____

_____

_____

_____

_____

What do I need to be aware of for my circumstances?

_____

_____

_____

_____

_____

Alimony (aka Spousal Support)

THESE ARE QUESTIONS THAT ARE CONSIDERED BEFORE AWARDING SUPPORT. MAKE NOTES ON YOUR CIRCUMSTANCES:

1. How many years have the couple been married?

_____

_____

2. Contribution to the marriage?

_____

_____

3. Income formula? Who makes who much?

_____

_____

4. Health of parties?

_____

_____

5. Earning ability and skills of each party?

_____

_____

6. Where Children are living?

_____

_____

7. Spousal waste or mismanagement of funds?

_____

_____

8. Who will be paying?

_____

_____

The Waiting Game

Can you practice the love you have for your kids and yourself MORE than the hate you have for your spouse???

_____

_____

_____

_____

Can you let go of the past and step into the light of the future life you deserve and desire?

_____

_____

_____

_____

Can you live in alignment with your best self and heal the old parts of you that wanted healing and validation from your spouse?

_____

_____

_____

_____

KIDS COME FIRST

When creating a parenting plan, consider some of the following points.

1. Does your parenting plan take into consideration the benefits of both parents' work schedules?

_____

_____

_____

_____

2. Driving distance between homes?

_____

_____

_____

_____

3. Do either of the parents travel for work?

_____

_____

_____

_____

4. Does it take into consideration the schedules and needs of the children? Their ages? Does it foster a strong bond?

_____

_____

_____

_____

5. Does it allow for ways to respectfully communicate?

_____

_____

_____

_____

6. Does it account for school vacations, summer vacation, holidays, Father's Day, Mother's Day, birthdays and special occasions?

_____

_____

_____

_____

LOOKING FORWARD BEYOND DIVORCE

How do you want to "Re-Define" you?

_____

_____

_____

_____

_____

_____

What do you want your new life to look like?

_____

_____

_____

_____

_____

_____

Who do you want to be?

_____

_____

_____

_____

_____

_____

CHAPTER SEVEN
REDEFINING SELF:
WHO DO YOU WANT TO BE?

Step Off the Spinning Wheel

JOURNAL YOUR THOUGHTS

1. How do you move on with your life when your mind is racing about the past?

2. How can you step onto a new path when all you see are roadblocks?

3. It's time to train your mind to LET GO.

4. You can't heal if you are still spinning your wheels and replaying your old story repeatedly.

ENERGY

Let your actions and habits do the speaking.

What are you emitting?

_____

_____

_____

_____

What is your home saying about you?

_____

_____

_____

What are your thoughts saying about you?

_____

_____

_____

_____

What are your friends saying about you?

_____

_____

_____

_____

_____

What are you saying about you?

_____

_____

_____

_____

_____

Reconnect and Reevaluate

THE NEXT STEP IS TO REEVALUATE YOUR PAST LIFE TO PREPARE FOR YOUR FUTURE LIFE.

1. Which relationships do you need to keep?

_____

_____

_____

_____

_____

2. Which relationships make you smile?

_____

_____

_____

_____

3. Which relationships can you and do you feel good about?

_____

_____

_____

_____

4. Which relationships are contributing to you being a better, more productive person?

_____

_____

_____

_____

5. Which relationships are in alignment with your values?

_____

_____

_____

_____

6. Which relationships are reciprocal?

_____

_____

_____

_____

_____

7. Which relationships are fun and loving?

_____

_____

_____

_____

_____

Make a list and write down how each person makes you feel and how they contribute to your life.

Person:

_____

_____

_____

_____

_____

_____

Person:

_____

_____

_____

_____

_____

_____

Person:

Person:

119

Person:

Person:

120

Person:

Person:

Person:

Person:

122

Now, it's time to do the same for the people in your life that don't do any of these things for you.

Person:

_____

_____

_____

_____

_____

_____

Person:

_____

_____

_____

_____

_____

_____

Person:

Person:

124

Person:

Person:

Person:

Person:

126

Person:

_____

_____

_____

_____

_____

_____

Person:

_____

_____

_____

_____

_____

_____

THE PEOPLE IN MY LIFE THAT NEED TO STAY AND GO

Keep

Let Go

1. Family

Keep   Let Go

_____   _____

_____   _____

_____   _____

_____   _____

_____   _____

_____   _____

_____   _____

_____   _____

_____   _____

_____   _____

_____   _____

_____   _____

2. Extended Family

Keep   Let Go

_____   _____

_____   _____

_____   _____

_____   _____

_____   _____

_____   _____

_____   _____

_____   _____

_____   _____

_____   _____

_____   _____

3. Old friends

Keep   Let Go

_____   _____

_____   _____

_____   _____

_____   _____

_____   _____

_____   _____

_____   _____

_____   _____

_____   _____

_____   _____

_____   _____

_____   _____

4.   New friends

Keep   Let Go

_____   _____

_____   _____

_____   _____

_____   _____

_____   _____

_____   _____

_____   _____

_____   _____

_____   _____

_____   _____

_____   _____

_____   _____

5. Work/Peers

Keep

Let Go

6. Professionals

Keep	Let Go

7. Neighbors

Keep

Let Go

8. Anyone else that sticks around

Keep   Let Go

What habits and patterns need to be re-evaluated?

Do you have negative habits or patterns because of people you associate with? Perhaps you need to let go of both the habit and the friend? Now you might think I am being cruel. I understand. You have some important decisions to make.

Keep a MONEY journal for 60 days to identify your relationship with money.

- Do you use money or does money use you?

- Do you take money for granted?

- Do you hoard money? Are you stingy or cheap?

- Do you spend it needlessly or to a point of irresponsibility?

- Are you in debt? How do you feel about being in debt?

- Do you have a financial advisory that you trust and speak to regularly?

- Do people owe you money?

_____

_____

_____

_____

- Do you owe people money?

_____

_____

_____

_____

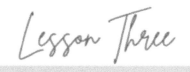

Explore All Your Possibilities

Have you ever given any thought to your hidden talents? Or exploring hidden talents that you never fully developed? Hint hint…you picked up the guitar but quit because you didn't have time…or your spouse told you that you didn't have the talent.

It is also time to revisit your old passions.

- What did you love to do that you stopped doing when you got married or took a job or had a child or moved?

_____

_____

_____

_____

_____

- What did you do when you were a kid that you miss doing?

_____

_____

_____

_____

_____

- What do you like doing that you stopped doing because you felt you didn't have time for it…like cooking or decorating or traveling or reading or going to the gym or running or… the list is long I imagine?

Lesson Four

Make Room for the New

WHAT ARE YOUR BIGGEST HURDLES HOLDING YOU BACK?

Here I go again asking you to journal your emotions and reasons for wanting to hold on.

_____

_____

_____

_____

_____

_____

What are you afraid of?

_____

_____

_____

_____

_____

Lesson Five

Dating in the Digital Age

Here are a few things to think about or journal to get clear on your emotions.

1. Sex in a new age. How does online dating feel to you?

_____

_____

_____

_____

2. NO one can tell you what is right for you. What is your gut telling you?

_____

_____

_____

_____

3. Sex is sex. Love is love.

_____

_____

_____

4.   What do you want? What do you need?

_____

_____

_____

_____

5.   Loving too soon! Time is a good thing. Give it time.

_____

_____

_____

6.   Get to know ALL about the other person.

_____

_____

_____

7. No one is perfect, but they should always be honest, kind and respectful.

_____

_____

_____

_____

8. When and how to introduce someone to the kids.

_____

_____

_____

_____

9. If you are the primary custody parent, it may be difficult for your new partner to "move in" for many reasons.

_____

_____

_____

_____

a. Privacy

b. Child support

c. Alimony

d. Rumors

e. Hurt feelings

f. Parenting conflicts

g. Your Ex's anger and jealousy

Lesson Six

Adventures In Freedom

What does the word adventure mean to you? I like to see adventure as learning to play again. Being willing to play again. **Wanting to partake in activities that bring you joy and a feeling of being alive.**

1. What does adventure mean to you?

_____

_____

_____

_____

2. Where do you want to go?

_____

_____

_____

_____

3. Who do you want to meet?

_____

_____

_____

4. Why do you want to go there?

_____

_____

_____

_____

5. Do you want to go alone or bring someone with you?

_____

_____

_____

_____

_____

_____

_____

_____

_____

GET OUT YOUR JOURNAL AND WRITE, WRITE, WRITE!

Okay …now tell me? What makes you excited? How do you find joy? Is it travel? rest? What makes you feel most alive? Can you finally give yourself permission to live life on your own terms and for no one else's agenda?

GRAB YOUR JOURNAL AGAIN AND LET'S CREATE YOUR BUCKET LIST.

How about we start with 50 things you want to do before 50? Or 60 things you want to do before 60? Whatever your age is…add 10 years and get writing!

1.

2.

3.

4.

5.

6.

_____

_____

7.

_____

_____

8.

_____

_____

9.

_____

_____

10.

_____

_____

11.

_____

_____

12.

13.

14.

15.

16.

17.

18.

19.

20.

21.

22.

23.

24.

25.

26.

27.

28.

29.

30.

31.

32.

33.

34.

35.

36.

37.

38.

39.

40.

41.

42.

43.

44.

45.

46.

47.

48.

49.

50.

51.

52.

53.

54.

55.

56.

57.

58.

59.

60.

61.

62.

63.

64.

65.

66.

67.

68.

69.

70.

71.

72.

73.

74.

75.

76.

77.

78.

79.

80.

81.

82.

83.

84.

CHAPTER 8:
KNOW YOURSELF

Create a Financial Future

A few things for you to consider.

1. Who will pay your debts after you die? (The goal is not have no debt)

_____

_____

_____

2. Who will pay for your burial or cremation?

_____

_____

_____

3. Who will inherit your assets? How will they be distributed?

_____

_____

_____

To Name Change Or Not To Name Change

This is a very personal choice.

- Is that something you are willing to hold on to?

_____

_____

_____

_____

- Is that something you are ready to let go of?

_____

_____

_____

_____

- Is that important to you?

_____

_____

_____

_____

- What is the advantage in your eyes of keeping your old name?

_____

_____

_____

_____

- What is the advantage of letting go of your old name?

_____

_____

_____

_____

- What is the new name you want to return to?

_____

_____

_____

_____

Goal Setting

Let's recall a time in your life when you nailed a goal.

- What was the goal?

_____

_____

_____

_____

_____

- When was it?

_____

_____

_____

_____

_____

_____

- Where were you?

_____

_____

_____

_____

- How did it make you feel?

_____

_____

_____

_____

_____

_____

_____

MIND MAPPING

Grab some colored pens. You can work in the book or on blank unlined paper.

Step 1. Turn to the next page and turn paper to landscape position.

Step 2. Write a word/idea that is a pressing issue in your life right now.

Step 3. Draw a circle around the word.

Step 4. Draw a line coming from the circle (like spokes of a wheel) with one word that comes to mind about the meaning of the word in the center of the circle.

Step 5. Continue to draw a line and write words until your mind is empty.

Mind Mapping

MIND MAPPING

THERE ARE THREE MAIN PARTS OF THIS WORK.

1. Dharma Code (a mission statement OR what I like to call the visionary statement of your soul)

2. Sankalpa: your short-term goal OR resolution that you can achieve within 6-18 months.

3. Vikalpa: your sabotaging behavior that always throws you off track from your desired outcome.

Let's celebrate our loves and passions!! What does that look like for you? Journal on your dreams for the future.

1. Moving?

_____

_____

_____

_____

2. Work?

_____

_____

_____

_____

3. Service?

_____

_____

_____

_____

4. Dreams?

_____

_____

_____

_____

5. Relationships?

_____

_____

_____

_____

6. Freedom?

_____

_____

_____

_____

_____

The Power of Healing

JOURNALING SPACE FOR

GRACE: **G**ratefulness, **R**elease, **A**cceptance, **C**hallenge, **E**mbrace

Gratefulness

_____

_____

_____

_____

_____

_____

_____

_____

_____

Release

Acceptance

Challenge

Embrace

Lesson Six

Celebrate Every Success

Take some time to get quiet. Take some time to sit tall, take a few slow deep breaths and contemplate where you were when you began this course and where you are now.

- Who am I now?

_____

_____

_____

_____

_____

- How am I different?

_____

_____

_____

_____

- Who do I cherish?

_____

_____

_____

_____

- Who cherishes me?

_____

_____

_____

_____

- What are my goals?

_____

_____

_____

_____

- How will I achieve them?

- What have I let go of?

- What do I need to prioritize?

- What am I most proud of?

_____

_____

_____

_____

- Who do I want to be in the future?

_____

_____

_____

_____

- How can I serve others?

_____

_____

_____

_____

- What are my gifts?

_____

_____

_____

_____

- What have I learned from this experience?

_____

_____

_____

_____

- How can I protect myself from making similar mistakes?

_____

_____

_____

_____

- What is my purpose in life?

_____

_____

_____

_____

Recognizing that change is a catalyst for growth, how do you measure each step?

_____

_____

_____

_____

Can you find an accountability partner?

_____

_____

_____

_____

How can you continue to commit to your own self-awareness, growth, knowledge and strength?

_____

_____

_____

_____

_____

_____

What skills do you now have that you didn't have before that can help you stay on track?

_____

_____

_____

_____

_____

_____

After you've gone through the five stages of grief, what is the lesson?

_____

_____

_____

_____

_____

Now it's time to reinvent yourself...what does that mean to you? Describe the new you. Describe your new life.

_____

_____

_____

_____

_____

_____

_____

NAME THREE ACCOUNTABLE GOALS THAT ARE VERY IMPORTANT TO YOU THAT YOU CAN ACHIEVE IN 6-18 MONTHS.

Goal 1:

_____

_____

_____

_____

Goal 2:

_____

_____

_____

_____

Goal 3:

_____

_____

_____

_____

Know your relationship patterns so you don't make a habit of repeating them. What are your patterns to watch out for?

_____

_____

_____

_____

_____

_____

How much of a priority is your healing?

_____

_____

_____

_____

_____

_____

How can you practice GRACE as you start your day every day?

_____

_____

_____

_____

_____

_____

How will you celebrate each small victory you achieve?

_____

_____

_____

_____

_____

_____

THANK YOU FROM MY HEART TO YOURS.

I thank you for taking this journey with me. I deeply thank Sonia Queralt, Casey Shevin and Tali Koss for sharing their legal brilliance and the power of Divorceify with me.

It is my desire that you feel a deeper sense of clarity, preparation and empowerment to thrive throughout the process of divorce. Know you are not alone. I am here to help guide and support you each step of the way.

Remember that private one-on-one coaching is always helpful. Just as each marriage is unique, each divorce is too.

If you found this book useful, please do take the time to leave a review on Amazon. This small step will help me reach and help more people just like you.

With thanks,

Paulette g. Rigo

PAULETTE RIGO

Paulette Rigo is a Mediator, Certified Divorce Coach, Trauma Informed Recovery Coach, Career Transition Specialist, E-RYT500, author of Better Divorce Blueprint the online course, book, planner and No Matter What card deck, Host of The Thriving in Chaos Project Podcast, Creator of Best Life Ever Retreats and founder of Better Divorce Academy, her commitment to creating an optimal divorce experience is her life's work.

It's Paulette's personal experience, high level guidance, resources and expertise that makes her continually strive to create a better way to divorce from the early stage of contemplation to the necessary final steps of healing using practical tools, inspiration and a proven road map for living out your dreams and desire to become who you were meant to be.

CONTINUING YOUR JOURNEY WITH ME

Schedule your private 45-minute consultation with me via www.betterdivorceacademy.com where the two of us can confidentially discuss what you need and how I can best serve you and your goals.

1. Luxury Exclusive Stand In The Fire With You Certified Divorce Coaching

2. Private 1:1 Certified Divorce Coach/Trauma Informed Certified Divorce Specialist

3. Sacred Space Inner Circle Closed Private Group Online Course, Coaching and Resources

4. Best Life Ever Virtual and Elite \Private Planning and Recovery Retreats

5. The Thriving In Chaos Project Podcast

6. Better Career Project Business and Book Creation Launch

7. Elite Confidential Mediation Services

8. Expert High Touch Master Mediation Divorce Team Creation and Resolution

9. No Matter What Inspirational Card Deck

10. Better Divorce Blueprint: The Book, The Journal and Eight Module Online Course

CPSIA information can be obtained
at www.ICGtesting.com
Printed in the USA
LVHW071912210521
688188LV00010B/605

9 781925 638721